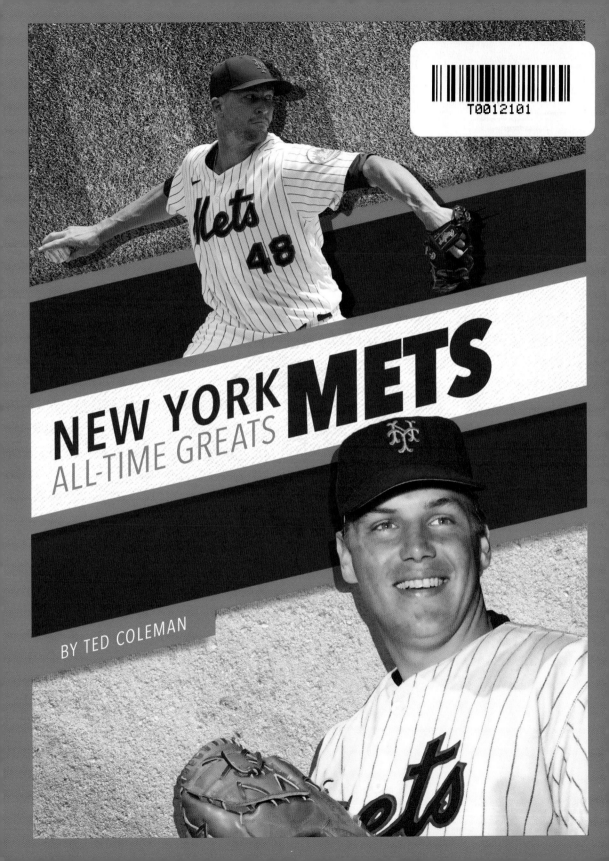

NEW YORK METS
ALL-TIME GREATS

BY TED COLEMAN

T0012101

Book design by Jake Slavik
Cover design by Jake Slavik

Photographs ©: Frank Franklin II/AP Images, cover (top), 1 (top); AP Images, cover (bottom), 1 (bottom), 4, 6; Harry Harris/AP Images, 8; Ron Frehm/AP Images, 10; Ray Stubblebine/AP Images, 12, 14; Larry Goren/Four Seam Images/AP Images, 16; Mark J. Terrill/AP Images, 19; Derik Hamilton/AP Images, 21

Press Box Books, an imprint of Press Room Editions.

ISBN
978-1-63494-505-9 (library bound)
978-1-63494-531-8 (paperback)
978-1-63494-581-3 (epub)
978-1-63494-557-8 (hosted ebook)

Library of Congress Control Number: 2022901758

Distributed by North Star Editions, Inc.
2297 Waters Drive
Mendota Heights, MN 55120
www.northstareditions.com

Printed in the United States of America
082022

ABOUT THE AUTHOR

Ted Coleman is a freelance sportswriter and children's book author who lives in Louisville, Kentucky, with his trusty Affenpinscher, Chloe.

TABLE OF CONTENTS

KRANEPOOL
7

CHAPTER 1
THE AMAZIN' METS

For many years, New York City was home to three Major League Baseball (MLB) teams. However, the Dodgers and Giants moved to California after the 1957 season. That left New York with only the Yankees. But in the early 1960s, MLB added several new teams. The New York Mets were one of them. They played their first season in 1962.

Unfortunately, the 1962 Mets were one of the worst teams in MLB history. They won only 40 games. The team had few stars. But by 1965, first baseman **Ed Kranepool** was playing at an All-Star level. He spent 18 seasons

SEAVER
41

with the Mets. During that time, he played 1,853 games. That's more than any other player in team history.

The Mets didn't improve much over the next few years. Back then, the National League (NL) had only 10 teams. The Mets finished 9th or 10th every year through 1968. But everything changed in 1969. That year, the "Amazin' Mets" won the World Series.

The team's excellent pitching led the way. **Tom Seaver** was one of the greatest pitchers in baseball history. The right-hander won his first Cy Young Award in 1969. That season, he won 25 games. Seaver went on to win two more Cy Young Awards during his career.

In the early 1960s, **Jerry Koosman** served in the US Army. He pitched for the team at the base where he was stationed. In 1964, Koosman signed with the Mets. And in 1969, he won two games in the World Series. Koosman pitched a complete game to clinch the championship in Game 5.

STAT SPOTLIGHT

CAREER WINS
METS TEAM RECORD
Tom Seaver: 198

JONES
21

Outfielder **Cleon Jones** joined the Mets in 1963. His best season came in 1969. Jones had an impressive .340 batting average that year. It remained a single-season team record for nearly 30 years.

Shortstop **Bud Harrelson** was never a strong hitter. However, he made up for it with his great fielding. After his playing career, Harrelson served as a coach and manager for the Mets.

Left-handed pitcher **Jon Matlack** joined Seaver and Koosman in the early 1970s. He won the Rookie of the Year Award in 1972. A year later, he helped the Mets reach the World Series again. This time, they lost in seven games to the Oakland Athletics.

The Mets struggled for the rest of the 1970s. However, catcher **John Stearns** gave fans something to cheer for. Stearns was an incredible athlete. The Buffalo Bills selected him in the National Football League (NFL) Draft. But Stearns decided to play baseball. He made four All-Star teams in 10 years with the Mets.

THE AMAZIN' MANAGERS

Despite being a poor team, the 1962 Mets produced three excellent managers. Gil Hodges led the Mets to the World Series title in 1969. Don Zimmer managed four teams during his career. Roger Craig won 738 games and took the San Francisco Giants to the World Series in 1989.

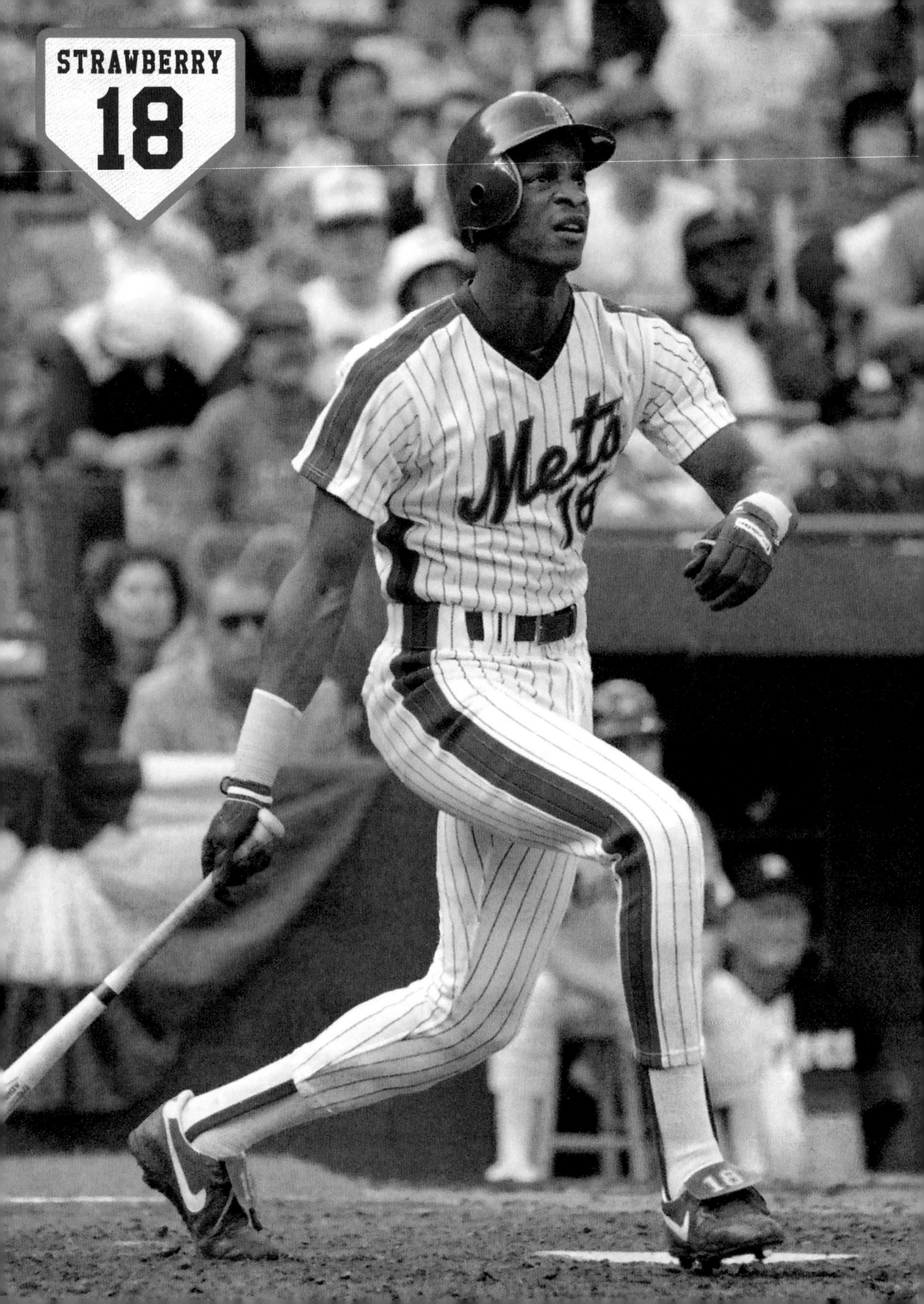
STRAWBERRY
18
Mets
18

CHAPTER 2
THE '86 METS

By the late 1970s, the Mets were one of the worst teams in the major leagues. However, they hired an excellent general manager in 1980. Frank Cashen had already helped the Baltimore Orioles win two titles. In New York, Cashen slowly put together the pieces of another championship team.

One of Cashen's first moves was to draft **Darryl Strawberry**. The tall outfielder had one of the best swings in baseball. In fact, some people compared him to Ted Williams. Many baseball fans consider Williams the greatest

GOODEN
16

hitter of all time. Strawberry didn't disappoint.
He earned Rookie of the Year honors in 1983.

Pitcher **Dwight "Doc" Gooden** made
his MLB debut in 1984. He was only 19 years
old. Even so, Gooden led the major leagues in
strikeouts that season. The next year, Gooden
had one of the best seasons of all time. He went

24-4 with a 1.53 earned run average (ERA). Not surprisingly, Gooden won the Cy Young Award.

Few people expected outfielder **Lenny Dykstra** to be a star. But Dykstra wouldn't take no for an answer. He was one of the toughest players in baseball history. Dykstra earned the nickname "Nails."

Cashen added a few more key players to make New York a true contender. In 1983, he traded for first baseman **Keith Hernandez**. And in 1985, the Mets brought in star catcher **Gary Carter**. Both Hernandez and Carter

MR. MET

In 1963, the Mets printed a picture of a mascot on their game programs. His name was Mr. Met. He had a human body and a giant baseball for a head. The next year, the team introduced a live version of Mr. Met. His popularity began a new era of live mascots in sports. To this day, Mr. Met remains one of the league's most popular mascots.

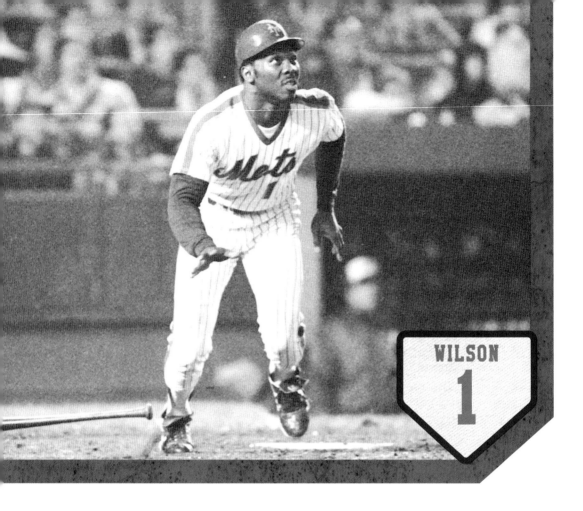

WILSON
1

were All-Stars at their positions. They were also intelligent leaders.

In 1986, the Mets made it all the way to the World Series. But in the 10th inning of Game 6, they were down 5–3. The Boston Red Sox were one out away from winning the series. Carter hit a single to keep the game alive. After another hit, third baseman **Ray Knight** came up. He singled to center field and brought Carter home. Now the Mets trailed 5–4.

Next up was **Mookie Wilson**. He had one of the most memorable at-bats in team history. A wild pitch flew past him, and the tying run scored. A few pitches later, Wilson hit a bouncing ball to first base. The ball went between the legs of Boston first baseman Bill Buckner. Knight scored, and the Mets won 6–5. It was one of the most incredible comebacks in World Series history.

Two days later, the Mets won Game 7. The team's fans hoped it was the start of a dynasty. However, New York made the postseason only once more in the 1980s. Still, the 1986 Mets are remembered as one of the greatest teams ever.

FRANCO
45

CHAPTER 3
THE MODERN METS

It took a while for the Mets to become contenders again. Throughout the 1990s, the team brought in many players who didn't work out. But one that did was reliever **John Franco**. The left-hander was a native of New York City. He was instantly popular with fans. Franco pitched 14 seasons for the Mets. During that time, he became the team's captain.

The Mets returned to the World Series in 2000. They faced the New York Yankees. The matchup became known as the "Subway Series." Unfortunately for Mets fans, the Yankees won the series in five games.

Catcher **Mike Piazza** was the heartbeat of the team. The slugger played eight seasons in New York. During that time, he cranked out 220 home runs. He also made the All-Star team seven times as a Met.

Left-handed pitcher **Al Leiter** joined the Mets the same year as Piazza. Leiter had bounced around the majors during his career. But he had his best years in New York. In 2002, he became the first pitcher ever to have at least one win against all 30 teams.

THE HEALING HOME RUN

The terrorist attacks of September 11, 2001, brought New York City to a halt. Just 10 days later, baseball resumed. Many fans at Shea Stadium were first responders. Others were families who had lost loved ones in the attacks. Mike Piazza hit a home run in the bottom of the 8th inning. The Mets went on to win the game. Many New Yorkers saw it as a moment of healing for the city.

REYES
7

Both Piazza and Leiter left the team in the mid-2000s. By then, the Mets had new stars. Switch-hitting shortstop **Jose Reyes** joined the team in 2003. A true speedster, Reyes was one of the most exciting players in the game. He led the NL in both triples and stolen bases in 2006. That year, the Mets reached the postseason again.

Next to Reyes was third baseman **David Wright**. Wright played his entire career with the Mets. He set team records in several categories. They included hits, runs batted in (RBI), and runs scored.

Outfielder **Carlos Beltran** was known for producing in the postseason. He hit three home runs in the 2006 National League Championship Series (NLCS). However, the Mets fell just short of another World Series appearance.

They made it back to the Fall Classic in 2015. But this time, they lost to the Kansas

STAT SPOTLIGHT

MOST CAREER HITS
METS TEAM RECORD
David Wright: 1,777

ALONSO
20

City Royals. The 2015 team was led by young, talented pitchers. Right-hander **Jacob deGrom** won the 2014 NL Rookie of the Year Award. He also won back-to-back Cy Young Awards in 2018 and 2019.

The Mets had another Rookie of the Year in 2019. First baseman **Pete Alonso** set an MLB rookie record with 53 home runs. Mets fans hoped the team finally had the pieces in place for another World Series title.

TIMELINE

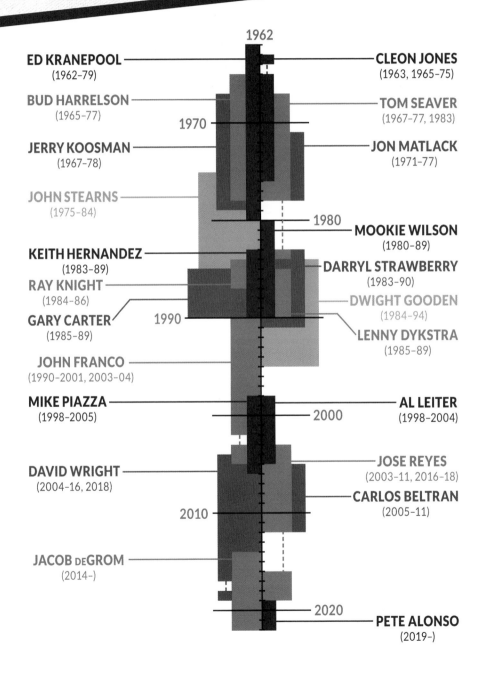

1962

ED KRANEPOOL
(1962–79)

CLEON JONES
(1963, 1965–75)

BUD HARRELSON
(1965–77)

TOM SEAVER
(1967–77, 1983)

1970

JERRY KOOSMAN
(1967–78)

JON MATLACK
(1971–77)

JOHN STEARNS
(1975–84)

1980

MOOKIE WILSON
(1980–89)

KEITH HERNANDEZ
(1983–89)

DARRYL STRAWBERRY
(1983–90)

RAY KNIGHT
(1984–86)

DWIGHT GOODEN
(1984–94)

GARY CARTER
(1985–89)

1990

LENNY DYKSTRA
(1985–89)

JOHN FRANCO
(1990–2001, 2003–04)

MIKE PIAZZA
(1998–2005)

2000

AL LEITER
(1998–2004)

DAVID WRIGHT
(2004–16, 2018)

JOSE REYES
(2003–11, 2016–18)

CARLOS BELTRAN
(2005–11)

2010

JACOB deGROM
(2014–)

2020

PETE ALONSO
(2019–)

NEW YORK METS

Founded: 1962

World Series titles: 2 (1969, 1986)*

Key managers:

Gil Hodges (1968–71)

339–309–1 (.523), 1 World Series title

Davey Johnson (1984–90)

595–417 (.588), 1 World Series title

Bobby Valentine (1996–2002)

536–467 (.534)

MORE INFORMATION

To learn more about the New York Mets, go to **pressboxbooks.com/AllAccess**.

These links are routinely monitored and updated to provide the most current information available.

*through 2021

GLOSSARY

captain
A team's leader.

debut
First appearance.

draft
An event that allows teams to choose new players coming into the league.

postseason
A set of games to decide a league's champion.

reliever
A pitcher who does not start the game.

rookie
A professional athlete in his or her first year of competition.

wild pitch
A pitch that the catcher can't reach, allowing a base runner to advance.

INDEX